This is the Way It Was

Growing Up in the Church of God

This is the Way It Was

Growing Up in the Church of God

Robert H. Reardon

Warner Press, Inc.
Anderson, Indiana

Published by Warner Press, Inc.
Warner Press, Inc.
Anderson, Indiana

All scripture passages, unless otherwise indicated, are from the King James Version or the Revised Standard Version, copyright, ©1972, Thomas Nelson.

Arlo F. Newell, Editor in Chief
Dan Harman, Book Editor
Cover by Larry Stuart

For Jerry and our kids:
Becky, Connie, Kathy and Gene

Table of Contents

Introduction

An old saying claims that a person who does not know, or understand, anything that happened before he or she was born, is an orphan. As I approach my seventy-second year, I have a thousand questions I wish I had asked my parents about the world in which they grew up. When I was young only the present interested me. But I suppose most of us come to a time in our lives when we are reluctant to have the experiences of our past buried with us.

For this reason I have tried to write about growing up in the Church of God. I want my grandchildren and others who might be interested to have some sense of what it was like to grow up in a world that never will be the same again.

The period of time involved runs from my birth in the Chicago Missionary Home in 1919 to the entrance of the United States in World War II in the early 1940s. It was a different world. Freud's theories of the subconscious were only beginning to plumb the depths of human behavior. The atomic age, civil rights, TV, World War II, Vietnam, Watergate, computers, and the quantum leap in space had not yet burst upon the scene to bring radical changes to our ways of thinking and living. I am reflecting on a quieter two decades between the two great wars, growing up in a midwestern town of 40,000 in central Indiana and a larger city, Denver, Colorado. But the setting is the kind of life I enjoyed in the home of a Church of God pastor and in the church.

Some Early Memories of Anderson

Our family moved to Anderson in the summer of 1920 from the Chicago Missionary Home. "We" were Eugene A. and Pearl Reardon, my parents, my brother Willard, grandmother Lydia Horman and her sister, Sarah Miller. Our house at 914 Walnut Street in Park Place was bought with a loan from grandmother, who had been given several thousand dollars by her brother, John Miller, founder of Chicago Tanning Company. He had struck it rich during the first world war, tanning hides that came from the great slaughter houses near the stockyards. The house had five bedrooms, was located three blocks from Park Place church and served us well.

The center of the universe for the "saints" was what father referred to as "The Office"—the Gospel Trumpet Company (now Warner Press). We were reminded of its presence by the siren that called the workers to the plant in the morning and released them in the late afternoon. Now that World War I was over, many were building small cottages on the campground in the area of the present Warner Auditorium dome.

After World War I, salaries and hourly wages began to be paid, and the former communal way of life was slowly disappearing. In the early 1920s E. E. Byrum was the patriarch: stocky, stolid, a no-nonsense elder statesman whose association with Daniel Sidney Warner went back to the early days of publishing in Grand Junction, Michigan. There he became part owner of the publishing company before it was reorganized. He succeeded Warner as editor, from which seat he had presided over the affairs of both the company and the church.

Now he had given the reins to F. G. Smith and had dedicated himself to the divine healing ministry, traveling across the church, both at home and abroad. He often spoke during testimonies in prayer meeting—a monotonous voice with a slight speech impediment. But he was a tough old bird, ready for action, the veteran of many a scrap. His brother, N. H. Byrum, held the purse strings as treasurer of the company. Most of the Anderson brethren called each other by initials, E. A., F. G., N. H., E. E., J. A., R. R. being common ones.

But the company was without question the heart, the energy center of the movement. Visitors entered the plant to see the great presses running, linotypes chattering, and thousands of books being bound and distributed to the ends of the earth with the message of unity, holiness, and heaven. They came away awed and inspired. The workers themselves were caught up in the cause and carried along in a sense of global mission. They were assured that God was working to restore the church and this entire enterprise was the vehicle through which it was being carried out.

Park Place Church

On Sunday the entire community worshiped at Park Place church—and father was the spiritual leader. He was the embodiment of Chaucer's description of the pastor-priest. His memory for names and faces was exceeded only by his love and intense interest in the congregation. He and mother worked as a team visiting the sick, those in trouble, the errant, and endlessly caring for the flock.

Park Place was never a typical church, even in the 1920s. It never was given to emotional extremes, with dignity and order the prevailing style of worship. Father was an impeccable dresser, scrupulously clean, dressed for the morning service in a Prince Albert coat and striped trousers. Our attendance ran in the twelve-hundreds—even so, few children got out without a hug and a very personal word.

One Sunday we were waiting dinner, and mother sent me out to find father. When I spied him he was sitting in a homemade wagon, his frock coat flapping behind, and his Bible under his arm, being pulled at top speed by the neighborhood boys.

One of the early Sunday morning services will be forever impressed on my mind. Seated on my mother's lap and not particularly interested in my father's sermon, I began squirming and kicking the back of Sister Sherwood's seat. She was not pleased. Mother's threats were to no avail and the ruckus caught my father's eye. He was not amused. He paused, closed his Bible, and as a thousand pairs of eyes watched, he walked down off the platform, lifted me firmly from mother's arms and headed for the vestibule. It was in the sanctity of

3

that south vestibule that I got my first instruction on what kind of behavior was appropriate in church. It was punctuated with several whacks that resounded clearly in the awful silence of the assembled saints. Sister Sherwood was pleased. After it was over, father carried me back to mother's arms, restored and in my right mind, whereupon he walked sedately back to the pulpit and finished his sermon.

Early on I had a strong aversion to church attendance. My beginner's Sunday school class was presided over by two important women Bessis Byrum and Birdie Smith, and I calmly reported to my parents that I would not go to Sunday school. To substantiate my decision I embellished it with the news that there were large, ferocious bears that prowled around the class, gobbling up a kid now and then. It was the little switch stuck behind the motto on the wall that read "all things are possible, only believe," that cured my twisted mind and made psychological counseling unnecessary. Not long after that I came in the house, my "pop gun" under my arm, to announce to my parents, "Come look. I've shot a piece off the moon." Some of my childhood friends have since made the unkind observation that this gift of exaggerated prevarication was the first shadowy indication of my future vocation as a college president.

It would not be fair to my father to indicate that he was a stern, sober, unbending puritan. There were two very central realities in his relationship to my brother and me; an abundance of love, which we felt daily in words, encouragement, and affection, and discipline, which formed the framework for it. It was no problem for us to think of

God as our heavenly Father who loves and disciplines his children.

In the early 1920s, father kept a checking account in the Anderson Bank and made a deposit of his allowance check personally. Here I met Linfield Myers for the first time when he took me along. Downtown was the center of county activity with stores surrounding the courthouse. Police walked their beats and father often stopped to converse with a passing officer and had me shake hands with him. Respect for the teacher, the police officer, the minister, was instilled in me from my earliest years. Church of God people were honest, respected the law, paid their taxes, prized the freedom to be a "separate people" and planned to keep it that way.

Those Interesting Characters

Park Place Church at that time housed some interesting characters. Brother Titley was a watchmaker. He used to sit on the south side, a green eye-shade on, and with an open Bible he appeared to read during the entire service. Once when father was preaching, he asked the rhetorical question, "Who made the sunshine? God! Who made the moon shine?" When moonshine was mentioned Titley suddenly came to life. "Praise the Lord, Hallelujah!" he shouted before father could answer the question.

Up front, behind the choir, the wall was covered with a larger than life mural of David the Shepherd. It had been painted in the 1920s by Ruthven Byrum, son of Noah, an artist who had studied abroad in Paris. It obviously had been drawn from a description in the Twenty-third Psalm. J. A. Morrison got in trouble with the Bryums by saying publicly that it was a good painting but that the shepherd's feet were too big. After that no one could look at the mural without wondering. Ruthven taught art at Anderson College for many years and during World War II was arrested in the mountains of Tennessee by a band of mountain people while painting one of his landscapes. They thought he was a spy.

During the 1920s Church of God people were serious-minded and wary of fun. Piety, sobriety, industry—"Every hour for the Lord let us spend"— was the way of life. There were strong prohibitions: no card playing, no drinking (prohibition), no movies, no smoking, no games on Sunday, no premarital sex. Social life was built around the church or an occasional class party or picnic. The more liberal ones indulged in a trip to Pendleton to swim in suits designed to let little sunshine in. But, I do not remember those days to be dark and somber. There was plenty of laughter and good times. We did peek over the wall on occasion. One of my buddies Fenton Flynt introduced me to *Uncle Billy's Whiz Bang*, a sort of racy publication that fascinated me, but Church of God people kept a watchful eye on us all.

In the 1920s there was no bobbed hair among saints at Park Place or anywhere else across the church. Women braided and twisted their hair into a spiral bun atop their heads. The style reminds me of pictures of the Tower of Babel in *Egermeier's Bible Story Book.* No revival or camp meeting was complete without a pulpit-pounding sermon aimed at worldliness—targeted principally at women who cut their hair, painted their faces, wore short skirts—and adorned themselves in a "worldly" manner. Mother had long, luxuriant hair that hung below her waist. Although its weight caused frequent headaches, she "came under" as Church of God discipline decreed.

This preoccupation with worldly dress came into the church from the Mennonites, large numbers of whom where drawn to follow D. S. Warner in the early days. The pastor's wife in Springfield, Ohio, was a former Mennonite and a highly influential example to women of central Ohio. Her pattern of life was strongly imposed on the women of satellite congregations who orbited around the Maiden Lane Church of God in Springfield. Women were supposed to look like Russian peasants—plain, unadorned, fully covered. When Lura Ann Farmer came to hold a revival for us in Denver about 1929, she was a shapely and attractive young woman who set our congregation ablaze with evangelistic fire. I overheard my father instruct mother to urge Lura Ann to modify her wardrobe a bit to dampen the fire.

Much thought was given in church circles during the 1920s to what was forbidden, and one's conduct was fairly carefully prescribed. Beside the Ten Commandments, for me there were such things as avoiding slang like gee-whiz, gosh, by golly, darn right—all judged to be only one step removed from blasphemy and cursing. Playing marbles for keeps, card-playing, movies, slot machines, and smoking were all temptations of the Enemy to lead us astray.

Repeated Repentence

Sliding and slipping caused me to repent many times—especially from playing marbles "for keeps" —"gambling," my mom said, "pure and simple," To make it worse, we had a sister in the church with a voice like an army sergeant who often favored us with a stern rendition of "There's an All Seeing Eye Watching You," a terrifying prospect for me after a good game of "marbles for keeps." Sermons on "Sin Can Never Enter There" had convinced me that eternal torment in hell-fire would be my lot for such transgressions. I often had to plead for forgiveness. This was all balanced off by a loving and understanding father whose faith was neither parochial or judgmental. So, I reasoned, the heavenly Father would be faithful to pardon my sin. But I often talked to God about things I never told my parents.

Although recreation among the saints in Anderson was fairly limited in scope, the "brethren" retired each week to the old dining hall on the campground for volleyball. I often went along and managed to swing from one ring to another and kick a huge medicine ball around while the sanctified smote the volleyball and, on occasion, had unsanctified words to say to each other.

It would be extraordinarily difficult for a college student coming to Anderson today to understand the isolation and separateness that existed between the church community and the city in the early 1920s. Looking over an old Park Place church photo of the congregation, I could not identify a single family that drew its income from other than Gospel Trumpet Company or the Bible Training

School. When one of the Gentiles appeared among us, they were easily spotted by dress, language, or smoke. Mother would say, "He is not one of our people." We drank not, smoked not, danced not, and mixed not.

We were thought by outsiders to be a peculiar people, separate by choice, and given to emotional extremes. That separation showed itself in isolation from community activities, service clubs, high school dances, and social events. Nonetheless the saints were well respected for industry and moral uprightness, particularly at Anderson Bank, presided over by its visionary president, Linfield Myers.

It is interesting to note that few, if any, college-age children of Anderson leaders attended the Bible School. This changed somewhat in the 1930s. The "be ye separate" message was strongly implanted in our psyche and few doors were open toward the city. This political separation finally was broken when Harold Achor ran for a Superior Court judgeship in the late 1930s and later when Earl Martin was elected a member of the City Council.

As I write this paragraph I am reminded of an 1988 June graduate for whom I wrote a reference to Indiana University Medical School. In the 1920s there were no medical school graduates among us. Our house at 914 Walnut Street had nothing in the medicine chest in the bathroom, not even toothpaste. Toothpaste was an extravagance. Salt and soda were better and cheaper. When there was sickness in the family there was the "prayer of faith" that heals the sick. Constipation might be treated with prunes but no patent medicine.

9

In the church, when there was sickness, father was the one called. He carried with him at all times a small vial of olive oil, which could be clipped on like a fountain pen. Father never held E. E. Byrum's theory of contract healing—if you met the conditions, God is contractually obligated to do his part. But bottles of medicine on the shelf in the 1920s were a sign of an absence of trust in God's power to heal. Such views often found their way to abusive extremes; lives were sacrificed, unhealed persons were forced to bear a burden of both illness, deformity, and guilt. With the exception of Christian Science, we were among the few teaching divine healing. One never can underestimate, however, the power of the healing message to attract new converts to our group.

2

The Gathering of Saints

Our memories of the 1920s and 1930s now must be viewed through the experiences of a half-century of change in the Church of God, the religious world, and the realities of the present era. The foibles, misreadings, and strange folkways are apparent; the history of the church in America is replete with narrowness and aestheticism.

Yet, this is not the whole story. Vivid in my memory is the electricity, the power, the sense of unutterable joy that were a part of our common life together in the church. There was a transcendent spirit of being chosen by God, empowered by God's presence to bring restoration and healing to an enfeebled and divided church. We knew who we were and what we were called to proclaim and do. We were dreamers of a great vision—a united, purified church, sanctified, empowered, global in purpose, reaching out, whatever the cost, to sound the trumpet of reformation before the end of the age.

Our services were times of rejoicing, weeping,

shouting, "waves of devotion" flooding our souls, "joy unspeakable and full of glory"—these were common with much of the same experience prevalent among the Pentecostals today, although "tongues" were not part of it all. It is this sense of purpose, of being God's chosen, of spiritual ecstasy, that so many of the older generation long for as they think on the past.

No place brought the saints together like the Anderson Camp Meeting, and in the early 1920s it was viewed as the spiritual center of the universe by Church of God people. In June pastors and laypeople made their annual pilgrimage to the "holy city" to celebrate, sound the reformation trumpets, to heal, evangelize, sanctify, purify the body of apostates and evildoers—and to feed on manna from heaven. To sit in the large tabernacle on wooden benches, sawdust on the floor, packed to the doors with an excited body of believers, caught up in great waves of thrilling songs—ready and waiting the exciting preaching of Riggle, Smith, Collins, Monday, Caudill—what an experience! Shouting, weeping, the service rolled on with a great rumble of amens when a point hit home.

Jerry's Conversion

My wife Jerry was saved as a ten-year-old in such a service. The PA system was extremely primitive, so only preachers with good lungs and heavy vocal chords could be scheduled to preach. In later years pioneer evangelist Walter Rimmer established himself on the immediate right-hand of the speaker to encourage him on. Once when the sermon was floundering he jumped to his feet and yelled at the top of his voice, "Hold still folks! He's bound to come to a good place pretty soon." Rimmer was known for his unorthodox methods of evangelism. His usual practice was to enter a strange town, find the fire alarm and ring it, preaching gospel fire to the gathering crowd.

Black people came to camp meeting in large numbers—sang reformation songs, shouted, mingled, voted, slept in the old dormitory, ate, and fellowshiped freely. This stirred up the townspeople, who protested to E. E. Byrum and others, but were not violent about it as long as this "insanity" was confined to the campground for one week a year.

Arthur Linn was the self-proclaimed "golden-voiced tenor" along with Rachel Lord who sang most often in the large services. Male quartets were very popular. They often ended with hands in the air, singing about the glories of heaven with saintly black Sister Cotton running up and down the sawdust aisles waving her white handkerchief and shouting the glories of God.

The old tabernacle, now Byrum Hall, the first to be built following the original tent, was constructed of hand-made concrete blocks. R. R. Byrum came from Moundsville as a young man, along with the other Byrums, to work on the new building. He told me that the window frames and stools were carted up from Moundsville and pointed to the steel girders that supported the roof—a declaration by the saints that no storm was going to be strong enough to blow it down as had the tent before it. The "acoustic bubble" on the north side of the tabernacle surrounded the speakers' platform and supported speakers, who sat in a semicircle, each with his finger in his Bible waiting for the Holy Spirit to give direction. I recall this building as a great place to sing. Sing, the saints did, until preaching time came. My father preached his first camp meeting sermon here, holding forth for fifteen minutes, although he said it seemed like an eternity. Once a more timid brother, unable to work himself up to any emotional outbursts, confessed to his disappointment in not being able to jump in ecstasy like the others. He was told to cross over into the graveyard and practice. This he did, on and off some of the lower tombstones.

The Indiana Railroad tracks came over from Muncie, through Yorktown, Chesterfield, across the river at Jackson's Crossing and thence cut through the campground and Maplewood Cemetery, on across the river near Truman Bridge and into town. It was an important link because it tied congregations in north, central, and as far as Terre Haute, Indiana, to the camp meeting. The interurban cars were electric motor driven, went sixty to seventy miles per hour, and had a horn blast that could be heard by the dead.

After World War II, when the campus was inundated with GI's and their wives eager to make up for lost time, they parked their house trailers around the gym, now Byrum Hall, because of toilet, shower, and laundry facilities. Morrison and Olt were alarmed because most of the young wives were pregnant and babies were arriving in large numbers. Dr. Carl Kardatzke, our resident sex expert, was asked to study this matter, which was hindering study habits of the students. I was in

President Morrison's office when the report came in. Carl said the first interurban came by at 5 A.M., with its horn blasting away, waking the GI's and their wives from slumber. It was too early to get up and too difficult to get back to sleep. So, he concluded, silence the horn and solve the population problem.

For a child, the main attraction at camp meeting was the lunch stand. It had a central spot on the midway with small frame cottages and booths crowded on the north side. Our old friend Steele Smith always was good for a nickel and I begged many an ice cream cone from him when I was six years old. Once in a while you could find a dime or quarter along the stand that someone had dropped. Candy bars were five cents and hot dogs were ten. The midway ran from the large tabernacle to Old Main, and at night it was a promenade for older teens having found each other.

Coming Back for Camp Meeting

After moving to Denver in 1926, the year revolved around our annual trip back to Anderson. We drove the long dirt roads across Eastern Colorado and Kansas, often in extreme heat or pouring rains that stuck most cars in mud up to the hubcaps. I can still see the jackrabbits jumping across Old North 40, caught in the beam of light from our headlamps—up and down, up and down the interminable road through Manhattan and Hill City. There being no motels and few hotels we could afford, we did what the saints did. We stayed with the saints. We ground up the miles one by one at forty miles per hour. Finally we concluded that the drive was like taking a dose of codliver oil—get it

15

over with as soon as possible—so we drove straight through, twelve-hundred miles, in a 1927 Nash.

For nearly everyone who came to camp meeting, it was about as close to heaven as one could get on earth. The great sea of people, the thrilling singing that could be heard from our house on Walnut Street, the sense of unity and power, the meeting and sharing with old friends, the excitement of hearing someone testify to a miraculous healing, the family bond, "our people"—"my people" feeling—this still exists in some ways even to this day. For one heavenly week no smoking, drinking, or using profanity—"O This is Like Heaven to Me," they sang. John Morrison took a somewhat jaundiced eye to the emotionalism of the services. He called it "whooping it up." It was not uncommon for those expecting a spiritual Utopia, as they walked from the Pennsylvania Railroad station, spying a smoker on the street, to be shocked. How could this be in Anderson?

The reformation movement was a great outburst of idealism. It was a call to return to the "early morning time"—to a church "without spot or wrinkle"—to a life of perfection and holiness, to a union of the saved and sanctified, drawn out of sin and the confusion of sectism. In many ways Anderson, headquarters of the Church of God reformation movement, was expected to be a reflection of these great ideals, and when the ideal met the real the discrepancies were hard to handle and difficult to explain.

I was not privy to the early GA meetings although I heard much from Dr. John Morrison and my father, who was the first chairperson. The original GA bylaws, setting up our initial concession to the need to conduct business in an "orderly manner," were straight out of the brilliant legal mind of F. G. Smith. Sessions required elections with results posted on the blackboard near the lunch stand for all to see. One year my father was relieved of his offices because of a painful, straightforward sermon on sectism among the saints. Conservative pastors, up in arms, gathered under the great trees gesticulating, warning, and arguing. The elections that followed were disastrous for father who was relieved promptly of his several national offices. When the GA convened again, all eyes were on him and the silence was electric when he rose to speak. "I have seen the election results." There was a long pause. "I have only one thing to say. The brethren gave and the brethren have taken away. Blessed be the name of the brethren!" Next year he was reinstated.

3

Memories of Yellow Lake

In the 1880s the holiness movement was sweeping across the land. It was largely energized by the writings of John Wesley and Charles Finney. D. S. Warner had not only been caught up in its claim that a second definite work of grace in the life of the believer was promised in the scriptures, but he had experienced this sanctifying presence of the Holy Spirit himself. It became a holy obsession for him. He wrote about holiness, preached holiness, and urged this experience until he was separated from the Eldership of the Churches of God. Not long after that he was convinced that holiness could never thrive in a sectarian denominational world. In October 1881 he stood up in a tiny country meeting house in Beaver Dam, Indiana, and declared himself to be forever free from human-made institutions, creeds, and unsanctified acts. It was in this unpretentious place that he took his stand with twice-born believers throughout the world. A handful of those present joined with him, and soon the message of salvation, holiness, and unity began to be heard in homes, school houses, brush arbors, and camp meetings. One of the first of these camp meetings was near Beaver Dam at Yellow Lake.

My memories of the Claypool campground go back to the earliest 1920s. The grounds were familiar to our family, my Aunt Edith and Aunt Marion having bought a cottage there shortly after World War I. It was next to a cottage that had been built for Nora Hunter. Her twins died in a flu epidemic that had swept through the land during 1906. They are buried at the cemetery west of the grounds. Also, nearby on the road was the Old Yellow Lake Bethel, the site where Warner established the Gospel Trumpet a few days before Christmas in 1880.

Mother brought me here when father and F. G. Smith made their year-long journey together around the world to study our mission work. Apparently I was a good baby. Mother often told me how I lay in my crib watching a colorful gourd swaying back and forth fastened to the end of a string from the ceiling. My head began to get flat on the back so grandmother took on the task of massage, trying to give me a proper round-shaped head like other babies. Yellow Lake cottages were lined up along the high bank, looking across one of Indiana's so called Kettle Lakes, left behind during the Glacier period. Our cottage had an attic for sleeping and a sleeping porch on the side.

In the center of the camp stood the old tabernacle. When our family lived in Chicago, we made a yearly pilgrimage, getting off the railroad at Claypool, where one could be hauled by horse-drawn cart the few miles to the campgrounds.

Straw ticks had to be filled from the huge straw stack in the barn, the cottage cleaned, and supplies secure from local farms set in. One year mother kept telling dad that something was moving around at night in their bed. After a great deal of reassuring, he finally took the straw tick outside and dumped it out. He was not amused to discover a large black snake had made its nest in the straw.

As time moved on, the saints determined to improve their toilet facilities. My Uncle Forrest Higgins, Brother Eli Gerig, and others, using old fashioned Hoosier ingenuity, devised an ingenious plan. Water from the lake was drawn to a large tank up on the bluff. Located directly across the road they constructed a new toilet facility. Connecting the tank and the toilets was a large wooden conduit spanning the road overhead. Inside the building the plan was simple and effective. It consisted of a low platform built over a trough; holes separated by a few feet. It was long on utility but short on privacy. When the pump completely filled the storage tank it tripped a valve sending a cascade of water across the conduit and down the chute into the trough. One had to be fairly spry when this happened to avoid the deluge.

No Swimming

The saints kept a watchful eye on campers. Bathing and swimming in the lake was strictly prohibited, but for the worldly some concessions were made. Bathing attire, consisting of Swedish blouses and calf-length bloomers for the women and girls, left everything to the imagination. Men wore tank tops and shorts below the knee. Suits would be put on in the cottage with robes or

21

clothing covering the prospective swimmer so that no skin was exposed to the naked eye. Then there was the drive out the gate past many a censorious eye to the other side of the lake, inhabited by the Philistines, to have our fun. It was referred to as bathing, since a good many of us took along a bar of Ivory soap. This was the high point of camp meeting for many of us children. So we sang:

"O me, O my, we'll get there bye and bye, If anybody loves camp meeting it's I, I, I, I."

I heard powerful warnings against John Barley-corn, smoking, tea and coffee drunkards, bobbed hair, short skirts, makeup, mixed bathing, movies, card playing. But never a sermon on gluttony. The saints ate very, very well.

Singing with the Saints

Camp meeting preaching was done by the most popular and dynamic preachers, black and white, men and women. Little attention was given to striking an even-handed quota based on geography, who had preached last year, or race. It was a festival of preaching and the church knew who they wanted to hear. Some who were bypassed made up for it in prayer, as Brother F. W. Chappel did . . . twenty minutes of prayer—including sermonizing and reminiscences of biscuits and honey at the old Kentucky cabin on the hill.

In the 1920s the country was in the midst of a revolution in church music. The German chorales and the Scottish psalm singing were imported by the immigrants. Later many of the hymns of Fanny Crosby, Frances Havergal, and Homer Rodeheaver became standard fare among all Protestant groups. They were songs of personal testimony in melodies familiar to the common person. In the Church of God we generally rejected "sectarian" things, but we never rejected its music. For the most part, songs by Church of God writers—Barney Warren, A. L. Byers, C. W. Naylor, D. O. Teasley, D. S. Warner—were lusty, spirited, rhythmic, and filled with scriptural imagery. Reformation theology was outlined particularly in *The Church's Jubilee* and *The Reformation Glory*. Because of heavy emphasis on doctrinal teaching and preaching we understood what we were singing about. Unfortunately few understand what they are singing about today in these songs, which are filled with biblical imagery.

Part singing was the hallmark of our congregational singing. New congregations, meeting in homes or storefronts, didn't need pianos or organs. Pitch pipes were common to get things started and often we would go from one song to another singing all verses by heart. This great musical tradition grew in part because it was one of the things approved and because of the excitement and emotional backing it gave our particular message. In nearly every case the congregation was the choir and we did not produce many musical performers in those days, save those I already have mentioned. Because of "end-time" theology, there were plenty of songs about heaven. Today we are in another revolution in Christian music, using popular and country tunes, choruses, and rock in some cases, which speak to the younger generation. Fewer and fewer heritage songs are learned or sung by the young—a sad prospect for the future, and the loss of a great bond between the generations.

4

Denver: A Mile High Feeling Fine

One morning, in the spring of 1926, mother came downstairs from her prayer time with a strong sense of direction. My brother Willard was not well, some thought it might be tuberculosis, and this was heavy on her heart. When she shared her sense that a move was in God's plan for the family, father said that he had been praying and felt led in the same direction. After camp meeting, we packed our clothing and utensils in trunks, strapped them on the running boards of the 1925 Studebaker touring car, said a tearful good-bye to friends, and headed west for Denver.

In the 1920s Denver was very much a rail and cow town. Heavy industry prohibited, the air was as crystal and clean as the driven snow. Mother, Bill, and I never had seen a mountain and expected as we approached Denver for the great towering Rockies to loom up suddenly into the sky. I recall the great disappointment as we caught our first glimpse—low on the horizon, unimpressive, distant. Of course this changed. As we drove into

Denver the brilliantly green lawns, the red brick houses, the snow capped mountains created a great sense of excitement.

The North Denver Church of God had fallen on bad times. Attendance was down, morale low, program in disarray. We were shocked to see young people eating ice cream on the back rows, sitting and talking out loud disrespectfully. I often have wondered what went through my father's mind. What a change from small town Anderson, Park Place, and the great headquarters church at Eighth and Union. I recall his telling mother that it would take five years to put this congregation on its feet. It took one week to stop the ice cream and the disrespect, and it was not long before the congregation knew it had a leader with high biblical standards of what the local church ought to be.

Ethnic Denver

Whereas Park Place church was the hub and center of eastside Anderson, the North Denver Church was implanted into a strong ethnic community of first and second generation Italian Catholics. In the first few months father made his door to door rounds of the neighborhood, only to discover how tough it was going to be to make inroads in this neighborhood. Certainly the saints thought they were bettering themselves to find a gothic-style building, magnificent stained glass, pipe organ and all for sale, cheap, from the Presbyterians who had fled. Unfortunately they had the pipe organ removed—an extravagant and sectarian sign of Presbyterian opulence.

Father's habit was to rise early, about five o'clock, read and pray in solitude, then go for a five-mile walk down Tennyson, past Elitch's, Berkeley Park, and home. Soon he knew the milkmen by name, along with other early risers.

School Days

When we moved to Denver in 1926 I was put in the third grade. It was a very unsettling experience since the Denver City Schools were far ahead of Anderson. I was lost and far behind, which led me to the conclusion I was a very poor student. I remember the inner terror of having to go to the blackboard to do math or to be asked to read the paragraph on the board. My parents soon realized the problem and I got lots of coaching at home; mother drilling me on the multiplication tables, father on reading. One semester I brought home all *D*s, which troubled my school-teacher father. I did not overcome my academic problems until the last years in high school, which has helped me realize that students develop in different ways and time frames, much of which depends on self perception.

In school in Denver when I was asked what church I went to, I said, "Church of God." Not one of my school friends had ever heard of it and no one in our neighborhood had heard of it either. This was a giant leap from the Park Place community where everyone knew of Church of God people. We sometimes forget how anxious children are to be a part of the standard-brand syndrome—speech, clothing, manners, heroes, and religion. There were no blacks in Edison Grade School, no Jews, but a strong contingent of Italians we called

27

Wops or Dagoes. They were all Catholics, stuck together in fights, and smelled of garlic. We were told that their mothers sewed their underwear on and they never took a bath. I had no reason to doubt that it was all true. But I was Church of God, went to a church no one ever heard of, and did not go to movies or play ball on Sunday, so I really didn't quite know where I fit. I used to dream about getting lost in school, winding up in the wrong room. One day my seventh-grade teacher made me stand up before the class and asked the class to tell me how I could be a better student. I never have forgotten the humiliation and what scars it left. I never told my mom and dad.

I am thankful for parents, particularly my mother, who always looked on the bright side, always was there with lots of encouragement day after day. She lit up the room with her sunny optimism and had the vibrant faith that "God works in all things for good." Serving the Lord as a pastor's wife, she thought to be a priceless blessing and opportunity. In my early years as a young pastor, and during my thirty-six years at Anderson College, I tried to show genuine affection for people and encourage them to believe in themselves and to support them in their quest.

Although most of my boyhood days were lived in Denver, far from the centers of population in the East, still we were caught up in the happenings of the day. Prohibition was not popular in the Italian-Catholic community, and even the people of German extraction were silent when the matter was brought up in church. There was a mood of optimism in the air. The war had made the world safe for democracy, and Charles Lindbergh's non-stop flight to Paris had inspired the country with the exciting possibilities of flight and given every boy an authentic hero. We drove downtown Denver and stood with thousands lining the streets as the open car with "Lindy" in it passed. Lindbergh, Babe Ruth, Admiral Richard Byrd, and Richard Halliburten were my heroes, along with missionaries like Grenfell, David Livingston, and Judson, and the great towering personalities of the Old Testament. Quite a distance from Michael Jackson, punk rockers, the Grateful Dead, and Sylvester Stallone.

When I was growing up, music was a big part of our lives and a major bond. Father, because of his responsibilities as worship leader in homes and other gathering places where no pump organs or pianos were present, had to learn to read the melody notes coming from reformation music published and circulated through the Trumpet Company. He had a strong, true baritone voice. Mother played the piano, Willard the cornet, and later, when about eight, I began taking piano lessons from Sister Carson, a member of our congregation in Denver. We always had an old Kurtzmann upright around, and gathering around to sing together was common. Mother's German tradition insisted that each child learn to play a musical instrument. I heard mother accompanying my brother as he played the "Holy City," the "Lost Chord," "Intermezzo" and other favourites in the classic and semiclassic tradition. There was no radio in the house in the early 1920s, and so we made our own music. My introduction to classical music came at Aunt Edith Mill's house, listening to the old Red Seal records on the wind-up Victrola. I also was impressed at the trademark of the dog listening intently to the gramophone and wondered what tune was being played. There were records of Percy Granger's *Country Gardens*, John Philip Sousa's Band, and favorite songs by tenor John McCormack.

Piano Finally Triumphed

Those early musical experiences led to a lifelong love affair with classical music. But learning to play the piano was something else while my buddies were outside calling for me to come out and play ball. When I began to play hookie from daily practice mother sat on the piano bench with me until I found some pleasure and excitement in what I was doing. Recitals scared me to death, waiting back stage wondering if I would break down in the middle of Paderewski's *Minuet*. Piano lessons continued through high school and study with Dr. Paul Breitweiser when we returned to Anderson. But when we went to hear the great organ in the Civic Auditorium in Denver, I never was the same again and determined that someday I would play a pipe organ.

When we returned from Denver, I was playing the piano rather well with a strong interest in the pipe organ. Alas, Park Place Church had no such instrument, but the idea of installing an organ became a persistent topic at the family table. Mother, Bill, and I came on strong, and finally father proposed the idea to the trustees. Fred Higgins, Stanley Funk, and Felix Wolfe reacted coldly to the idea, whose time they thought had not come. So father got a promise from them to

30

okay the project if the money could be found elsewhere. In no time the young people had a campaign going, raised the money, and Wickes Organ Company found a suitable instrument, rebuilt it, and installed it above the baptistry. Before it could be dedicated and put in use, Felix Wolfe moved at a business meeting that *nothing* but "hymns and spiritual songs" be permitted to be played on it. Fortunately the motion lost.

Until the new instrument was available I began to study the organ with Mallory Bransford, practicing on the organ at First Christian Church. Mallory was a graduate of Oberlin Conservatory and the son of Dr. Bransford. The sanctuary was cold and mother fixed a hot-water bottle for me to carry along with my music when I went to practice. I am sure that Mallory Bransford influenced my decision to spend a summer at Oberlin in 1938 studying the organ with Arthur Crowley, whose mentor in Paris had been a student of the great Cesar Franck. I played regularly in church until I went to Oberlin for seminary training in 1940. This skill enabled me to secure the position as chapel organist in Fairchild Chapel, which paid for my tuition and most expenses during my three years there. Many years later I sat down at the magnificent organ in the ancient eleventh-century State Lutheran Church near Hibben, Germany, where my mother's ancestors had worshiped and played Luther's great hymn *Ein feste Burg*. It was a special moment.

5

Money—The Absence of It

I find myself coming back to the subject of money, a subject of more interest to mother than dad. Perhaps it came from her own instincts as a businessman's daughter and her inclination to be aware of what money could provide in food, clothing, books, music, for the family. Dad never spoke of a salary. Salaries were paid in the secular world. People traded skills for services rendered. It was totally different in his world. His ultimate commitment, all, everything was God's. It was given freely in response to Christ's gift of forgiveness and love. His life, money, talents, time were dedicated to God and what he received he referred to as his "allowance" rather than his salary or paycheck. Allowance for him was a part of God's kindness in providing for living expenses, caring for family needs. I honor him for this. Most of us have distanced ourselves rather considerably from where he was at that time.

Growing up I never thought of ourselves as being poor. I did wear hand-me-down clothing and we drove an old car, but the depression was on and we had considerable company. An allowance of twenty-five cents a week wasn't much even then, so I turned to other devices to satisfy my needs. I was the best marble-shooter in the neighborhood and shot the other boys out of their hoard, which filled several cigar boxes. This was my currency I used to trade for things I wanted, and I became a very good businessperson, early on.

Being of a somewhat inventive mind, I decided to do something about the disreputable old 1926 Nash we were driving. My ears picked up when I heard the Creamo Cigar commercials on the radio. They advertised a contest in which a new 1929 Plymouth—floating power—would be given for the best fifty-word essay on "Why I Smoke Creamo cigars." All entries had to be accompanied by twenty Creamo cigar bands.

The prospect of winning a new Plymouth set me on fire and for weeks I checked the precincts around the cigar store across from Elitche's Gardens. When I finally had the qualifing number, I went to work and, after many drafts, came up with what I thought to be an inspired account of the indescribable pleasures of smoking Creamo cigars. This I mailed in and watched each day for the mailcarrier and prayed each night to win. It was for a "good cause," I said to the Lord, which seemed to salve over the slight uneasy feeling in my conscience. Alas, the days passed and I never heard. Someone else was driving the new Plymouth. As I reflect on my father's impassioned sermon on "Twelve Reasons Why Smoking is a Sin," I probably was better off not winning.

Church of God people seemed to have nothing against firecrackers although I was warned by father that this particular year, about 1928, I was not to purchase any firecrackers over two-inches long. I did not purchase any. That satisfied the law. But, I reasoned, I did not promise to trade for any of larger size. I got a six incher for fifty marbles and gathered my neighborhood buddies to watch me blow a tin can out of sight in the alley behind our house. Believe it or not, we could not find a can. The trash collector had just made his weekly pass, but I found a one-quart Mason glass jar. Soon I got it all set. The punk was ready to light the fuse when my dad happened to look out the back window and see what was about to happen. It was one of the few times I heard him yell. "Stop! Stop!" he cried, as he came running toward me, his face white with alarm. "Don't you know what you are doing? You might have blinded yourself for life!" It was not my best day.

6

Baptism, Foot Washing, and Meanness

In the 1920s getting saved was the way one came into the Church of God. Generally a convert turned away from the past life of sin and rebellion and responded by confession at the public altar. In our revivalist tradition the experience was a major reorientation of life, accompanied by sincere outbursts of emotion and joy. Preachers often talked about a "know so" religion and about being able to identify the exact time and place it all happened. Being raised in a devout family I was taught that sin was evil in God's sight, and when I did wrong I was to confess to God, the heavenly Father, and ask for forgiveness. Often praying before bedtime I would ask for God to forgive and save me. So, as a child, and being fearful, I never was drawn to the church altar until I went to high school, but I sometimes felt that I should have been as we sang during the altar call

"O sinner heed the Spirit's voice,
This call may be the last."

It was written by my father in 1907 but, even though kept in our hymnal for years, I never heard him use it. But when asked about my soul I gave an affirmative reply. "Yes, I loved the Lord. Yes, he forgave me. Yes, I was committed to serve him all my life." This apparently was good enough for baptism.

When I was ten I was baptized and went to my first foot washing. Not until later did I realized that foot washing was not a universal practice among Christians. This was something we referred to as an ordinance and practiced because after Jesus washed the disciples' feet, he said, "Blessed are ye if you do these things." So, we complied. Men and boys gathered separately, sat in a large circle, took off shoes and socks till another came with a basin of water and a towel. After the washing, both stood and embraced. This was an uncomfortable experience of questionable meaning to me until I saw, during my high school years, Dr. John Morrison kneel and wash our janitor's feet. Then I realized the profound symbolism inherent in the ceremony.

Unfortunately, in the early days, washing the saints' feet became a test of fellowship. One of our finest pastors, W. F. Hopkins, was set aside, when I was a child, because he did not agree. Sometimes during foot washing there was some looking around to see who was absent, a kind of judgment that the absent ones had not gone "all the way" and were holding back.

Drama and Laughter

Since drama was closely tied to worldliness and the theater, there was not much of it going on in the church. I recall vividly one occasion, however.

It was an Easter pageant staged on the platform of our church on Vallejo Avenue. A screen had been devised by drawing a wire across the front and an elaborate set had been constructed with a tomb surrounded by ferns and flowers. When the curtains opened I was more than impressed to see dear Sister Ingram, dressed in a white bathrobe, complete with attached wings, make an angelic exit from what looked for the world like the two-hole privy at Berkley Park, announcing in an angelic voice, "He is not here. He is risen." My outburst of laughter somewhat spoiled the general spiritual impact, and with the speed of light, mother had me shoved under the pew.

Many things happened in those solemn days that were not supposed to be funny but were rich with whimsical humor. Father had a hearty laugh but never told anything funny in the pulpit. I was first attracted to Dr. Morrison as a boy because he always could be counted on to say something humorous in his sermons. During one of his illnesses, he came to Denver and lived with us for a month but fell ill with homesickness and hurried home.

When we arrived in Denver in 1926, mother realized that she had a cousin Lillian, married to one of Denver's most distinguished businesspersons, John Zahn, treasurer of the Portland Cement Company. In due time we were invited to their handsome apartment over on Ogden Avenue for dinner. I never shall forget the exquisite table, set with sterling silver and lovely china. My downfall came trying to manage the tall-stemmed crystal goblets, which I knocked over three times. It was a wet meal for us all and a bad time for mother. We did go back from time to time, however, and father was carried away with John Zahn's remarkable collection of first editions, a classic and valuable literary treasure. But the Zahns, though warm friends, moved in different circles than we, and their adherence to Mary Baker Eddy added to the distance.

The houses on our block all had identical garages with windows on each side so, lined up as they were, one could look through several of them far down the block. It was spring but in spite of being a warm day there were some remaining piles of wet snow around. I happened to peer through the garage windows and whom did I spy but our neighbor Mr. Miller, a fiesty young man with a quick temper, out painting his garage—a bucket of paint in one hand. Being relatively hidden by several garages between us I made a fine snowball and gave it a long toss over the roof and checked to see how close I'd come. Bull's-eye: The missile landed squarely on target, knocked off Miller's hat, jarred the paint bucket out of his hand, and altogether disrupted his painting project. He was boiling mad and it took him only a split second to come charging after the culprit. I made a bad strategic error and began to run at top speed down the alley but, alas, he was faster, caught me, pinned me on my back to the ground, sat on me, and painted my face perfectly white— ear to ear. It took mother and turpentine hours to clean me up and worst of all was a trip down to the Millers to apologize afterward.

I think I would not be characterized as a bad boy growing up on the north side in Denver, but I was no paragon of virtue either. One evening one of the older roughnecks in the neighborhood enticed me into a project that could have had unfortunate results. He had me cup my hands and make a lift for him to peek into the neighbor's bedroom. He did not report having seen anything interesting, but I became more uncomfortable and decided to head for home. It was already dark and, like God seeing Adam in the cool of the day, father already was out looking for me. I did not exactly lie to him about what had been going on, but neither did I tell him the truth. Both he and I sensed that something was amiss, but it never came to light.

Often during those days mother would repeat her oft-used line, "tell me who you go with and I'll tell you who you are." The bonding between me and my parents was strong, and anything that threatened that relationship was always troublesome for me. As I look back I am confident their love was unconditional, but I was not mature enough to understand that. I was sure that if my father knew what I had been up to, he might somehow not love me anymore. In more than thirty years of dealing with college students in trouble, I have observed they will go to virtually any lengths to keep their parents from knowing when they are into heavy wrong-doing.

Photos on page 43

1. Eugene A. Reardon.
2. The Church of God Missionary Home in Chicago, 1920.
3. Bob with Mom, Pearl Horman Reardon.
4. Bob, E. A., Pearl and brother Willard, about 1930.
5. Father and sons, 1923.
6. The family, Anderson, 1934.

Photos on page 44

1. Outside Anderson Tabernacle, about 1930.
2. Inside Anderson Tabernacle, about 1920.
3. Russell R. Byrum, John L. Phelps, Bessie Hittle Byrum, J. T. Wilson, H. C. Clausen.
4. F. G. Smith, E. E. Byrum, C. E. Brown.
5. A. F. Gray.
6. Anderson campground bookstore, about 1930.
7. H. M. Riggle, N. H. Byrum, E. E. Byrum, B. E. Warren, A. T. Rowe, E. A. Reardon.

Photos on page 45

1. Young Bob on his trike, 1925.
2. In the yard, 1920.
3. In Denver, 1930.
4. With friend.
5. Bob and Bill, 1925, Anderson.
6. With Galen Smith, 1923.
7. H. S. senior with '36 Studebaker.
8. H. S. sophomore, 1934, Anderson.
9. Dating, 1939.

Photos on page 46

1. At Oberlin, Graduate School of Theology, 1941.
2. Organist, Fairchild Chapel, Oberlin.
3. At Anderson College, 1939.
4. Wedding, 1941; left to right, top: Jack Van Dyke, Carol Helvey, Lois Denton Church, Janelle Boger Mittan, Jean Reynolds Newberry, Willard Reardon, Jerry and Bob.
5. With President John A. Morrison.
6. With Dean Russel Olt.

7

Love and Discipline

Early in the Denver years, father thought that military discipline would be good for me. I was signed in as a Highlander Boy, a kind of military academy with weekly drill and instruction. Although cadets, we lived at home and attended public school. I was issued both an army and a navy uniform, World War I variety, a look-alike army rifle, and other gear. To be issued a regulation uniform, I had to be measured by one of the officers, an ex-army World War I sergeant, who took out his tape, read me up, down, across, then paused and solemnly announced that one of my shoulders was a half-inch shorter than the other. Deformed, I thought. What a blow!

Tears filled my eyes as I rode home on my bike. To think that I shall have to live all my live with this handicap. I already had been teased about having big ears; now this also. It was almost too much to bear, but it was not until months later that I finally had the courage to tell my father, who assured me that no one had perfect shoulders and, that as I grew larger and taller, my ears would blend into perfect harmony with the rest of my body. What relief to feel normal again. Most of our training was regular drilling, camping, competitive sports, and other events designed to instill discipline, patriotism, and a code of honor.

In the summer, several thousand of us gathered each week in the city park to march, accompanied by our own bands and applauded by our parents. My first time away from home was a week-long camp, just outside Estes Park in the mountains, where we pitched our tents, slept in cots, and lived military fashion. I became desperately homesick, despondent, and miserable but managed to stick it out. But there were some moments. I still can recall the great campfires at night, a thousand of us singing under a crystal-clear night full of stars, surrounded by the great towering Rocky Mountains:

"Moon, Moon, Great Big Silvery Moon...,
"John Jacob Jingle Heimer Smith."
"Hinky, Dinky, Parlez Vou."
"It's a Long, Long Way to Tipperary,"
and other World War I songs. The final Saturday I was feeling better and ate thirteen hot dogs for lunch. I was starved. It was a feat I never have been able to duplicate.

As I reflect on my father's enthusiasm for my military training, I think how nearly absent from our church was the "peace witness" so central among the Mennonites. World War I, the establishment of the League of Nations, a world safe for democracy, the solid support of the military by the country in the war effort—this was generously accepted by Church of God people.

The Pain of Growing Up

Perhaps it was father's experience as a young school teacher in Bellefontaine and Urbana that convinced him his boys would not be a part of the unruly bunch. Get a lickin' at school; automatically you got one at home. Early on the rule was "come when you are called; don't talk back." If you slam the door, come back and close it quietly. Say "excuse me please" if you had to leave the table. Eat with your mouth closed. Don't smack your lips. Don't talk with your mouth full. Never belch at the table. Wash before you eat. Answer "yes, ma'am," "no, sir" to your elders. Be sure to wash your ears. Father regularly examined my ears and I can hear him say, "I could grow potatoes in those ears!"

Punishment for wrong was immediate and most generally fit the occasion. One hard and fast rule was that I had to understand why. The second was that it was never administered in anger. Several occasions come to mind. Playing in the alley with older boys I heard some electrifying words that I did not understand at the time. Once when our friends, the F. G. Smiths, came for dinner I called my brother a bastard. The whole world suddenly stopped; I was led quickly from the table. Father did realize that I had said it in innocence and I was spared somewhat, but after a good lecture I had my mouth washed out with soap.

Serious offenses called for a private confrontation in his office. There in the basement of our house on Moncrieff, bookshelves lined the walls. A large desk stood at one end of the room with a map of the world on the wall behind and an old leather couch along the wall. It was here that it all came out, a strong lesson on right and wrong followed, and then the razor strap. I shall never forget the impact of these rare occasions. The tears that flowed, the humiliation I felt, the pain endured, were all very real—but there was something else.

After it was over, he and I knelt by the old couch for prayer of confession and forgiveness. When we had both prayed it was over, but not quite. When we stood up and faced each other, there was a kind of awkward silence, for it was not yet all over: he never failed to reach out his arms to me to hug me tight and tell me how much he loved me and what kind of man he hoped someday I'd be.

The pain and humiliation has faded with now more than sixty years, but I still can feel his arms strong about me and his love. This I shall carry with me to my grave. When the junior and senior high years came, discipline took other forms, but the elements of punishment, reconciliation, and love continued, When I reflect on these experiences I thank the Almighty for a father who understood the redemption power of discipline, love, and reconciliation.

Father had a passion for improving things. Buy a used car and improve it, make the church shine with new paint, clean out the trash, get the saints organized for action, improve the bylaws. As a pastor he had no equal. Pastoral visits were a serious occasion for church families gathering in a circle in the living room. An update was given on each member—school, work, problems, sickness; then down on their knees and a pastoral prayer for each member by name and a hug for the children before leaving. Such care built the North Denver church to health in due time although not a single ethnic neighborhood family was won in the seven years we lived there.

Old-Fashioned Revival Time

Two revivals of two weeks each were held each year. Father was not a fiery evangelist and knew that there was an appetite in the church for various kinds of preaching. Strangely enough, he brought country folk preachers like Paul Bennett from rural Missouri; Harvey Pinyoun, young dynamic ball of fire from Canada; Harvey Wright, cowboy preacher; J. W. Lykins, southern orator with his hair-raising stories of the awful tragedies that befell those who rejected the altar call.

No doubt some responded because of their hunger for God. Others responded because they were scared. Revival services never were a spiritual retreat. They dealt with the reality of sin and its consequences, the fragile nature of life, the reality of hell fire and eternal punishment, and the need of Christ's atoning, cleansing blood, to save one from sin. At the public altar sinners humbled themselves and came to receive God's forgiveness and grace. There, surrounded by the community of faith, one was born again and became a part of the church. It was a place where emotions ran deep and salvation was a cause for "joy unspeakable and full of glory."

When I was thirteen I was conscious that there were other heavenly places.

The length of mother's long hair, which fell to her waist, caused other problems besides regular headaches. Near our house at 4627 Moncrief, in North Denver, was a nationally known amusement park. Elitch's Gardens was known for its magnificent dahlias and its terrifying roller coaster. Since mother was interested in the former, and my brother and I in the latter, we schemed to entice her into this den of iniquity one week while father was away. After patiently observing the flowers, we guided mother to the roller coaster.

After a lengthy pleading and assurances of pleasures and safety mother agreed to go, with the provision we go together and that she choose the seat. We were pleased when she chose the first seat. I can still recall the long ascent to the top of the first incline—highest, they said, west of the Mississippi. Mother's fears were put to rest as we ascended upward with a fantastic view of the city and the Rocky Mountains to the west.

Then for a moment we hung over the abyss, followed by a real gut-wrenching dive downward, passengers screaming, holding on for dear life. On and on we went, skyrocketing upward, plunging downward on this hair-raising ride. I looked at mother. Her hairpins had come loose, and her hair was streaming out behind, and she was crying to the Almighty for mercy. We led her, somewhat shaken, to a quiet place after the ride finally was over. There she swore to God that never, no never, would she ever put herself into such a contraption of the devil again. She never repeated this experience to father.

When Al Smith ran for president, I heard him speak from a truck bed in downtown Denver. It was covered with slogans and colorful bunting. Church of God people were driven into the Republican fold because, they argued (a) Smith was a Catholic and if elected we would be governed by the Pope; (b) he was against prohibition. Father had a keen interest in what was going on in the marketplace, read the *Literary Digest,* the *Denver Post* and *News,* and, on occasion, spoke out from the pulpit on such matters.

Again, it was the world out there—full of sin and wickedness—from which we needed to be saved. Heaven was our home. But when you are a ten-year-old boy, fascinated by what went on, on the other side of the mountain, it was not easy to keep your mind on heaven. What, I wondered, really went on in theaters where movies were shown? Later when I was a high school sophomore, Fenton Flynt and I broke over and sneaked into a Sunday afternoon movie. When mother heard about it she took to her bed for two days, saying that I had ruined my father's influence and had brought shame and reproach on the "cause," a phrase used in our home for the reformation movement. Few things could be more devastating. It was not the only time I made mother suffer.

Tough Days in Denver Schools

All the seven years we lived in Denver there was a subtle feeling that we were ex-patriots. But those were formative years for me. I was trying hard to catch up from the old Park Place School where the Park Place church now stands. Standards were a serious level higher in Denver, which nationally was known for its excellent school system. I was badly behind in reading, so father assigned a different psalm for me to read each day when our family gathered for worship. I shall eternally be thankful for this. The majesty of King James English, the imagery of language, the sublime insights of the psalmist came on to impress me, slowly at first, father helping out with difficult words and phrases—but after several years the effect grew stronger and deeper.

In my preaching today I find myself using frequent verses and phrases that became a vital part of my life early on in those years. Besides this, there is no finer benchmark for excellence in English language, and whatever writing skills I might have acquired, I credit to a familiarity with biblical poetry and prose.

Bible reading at worship was followed by a chapter in *Egermeier's Bible Story Book* in the evenings. Particularly the stories of heroism, war, violence, victory, and defeat of Israel's armies enthralled me. These great epics, woven into the fabric of my life as a child, stood me in good stead for the much feared middlers Bible exam in seminary. We Church of God students, Warren Edmondson, Gene Newberry, John W. V. Smith, and Irene Caldwell, passed with flying colors. Those with "liberal" backgrounds did not do well.

The crash of the stock market in 1929 had little effect on Denver for the first few months, but later its effect was devastating. The effect on our congregation was dramatic. In response to the endowment campaign for Anderson College, the North Denver congregation was organized and prepared. A huge banner was stretched across the sanctuary, promoting the effort, and my father's devotion to education in general and to the college in particu-

56

lar came through loud and clear. Alas, the crash brought banners down all across the country.

During those tragic years that followed, most of the men in our church were out of work, discouraged, apprehensive, with no federal or state programs available to help. But the church came together as a family. Food and clothing were shared, needs were met—and the bonding together of families increased day by day. Sundays and prayer meetings reinforced our need for each other and our need of God's presence and promise of hope. Even though I was a boy, this period of time had a profound effect on me, sitting with mother, surrounded by the saints, people we knew and loved, hearing her lead off with

> 'Tis so sweet to trust in Jesus,
> Just to take Him at His Word,
> Just to rest upon His promise,
> Just to know, "Thus saith the Lord."
>
> Jesus, Jesus, how I trust Him!
> How I've proved Him o'er and o'er!'
> Jesus, Jesus, precious Jesus!
> O for grace to trust Him more!

The saints got up off their knees, eyes shining, faces glowing with renewed hope. It was indeed the family of God! It is a strange paradox, but the North Denver Church never was stronger than in the depths of the depression.

Survival was the name of the game in 1930-31. Mother's oft used expression was "when our ship comes in," or using her German would say, "*So ghet, wen Frau und Kinter hat.*" Father's was "we pay as we go or we don't go." But after months of skimping and hoarding every penny I finally had twenty-five dollars—enough to buy my first bicycle, a twenty-eight inch Hawthorne, second-hand Montgomery Ward model. Coming home from Skinner Junior High, I made a fast turn on loose gravel, lost it, and slid under a car that, fortunately, was braking for a stop sign. Prayers of thanks were offered that night at worship for sparing my life.

Grandmother lived with us in Denver, along with her sister, Sarah Miller, who for years had been a matron of the Chicago Missionary Home. Both had a tendency to start their prayers in the Garden of Eden and end on the Isle of Patmos. Grandmother Horman and Aunt Sarah carried much of the housework, freeing mother to go along with dad to make house calls—an average of more than one hundred per month. Mother went along for two reasons. She was full of light, optimism, and good will. Going into the home of a shut-in, she was apt to sit down at the piano to play and sing some encouraging songs. Second, father loved her company and, besides, there was no home they could not enter at virtually any time of day or night. No breath of scandal ever came near father's door.

Dad never cheated Bill or me of time. He taught me how to throw a baseball and swing a bat, how to ice-skate down at Berkley Park, how to ride a bike, how to swim and drive a car.

8

The Facts of Life

Father was a great teacher and had a wide-ranging vocabulary for nearly every subject but sex. I recall vividly the walk together down the sledding hill on Vrain Street when he broached the subject. I was twelve and about as naive and uninformed as a youngster ever could be. After a long silence he explained briefly that babies grew in a mother's body and that the man, well sort of, entered the woman.

His mission accomplished, we went on to other subjects with which he was more comfortable. It was an intriguing walk that opened a whole new horizon but left me with a thousand mysteries. In those days in the church no one ever spoke publicly about sex. My parents were affectionate and obviously very much in love. Father found mother wherever she was in the house to kiss her good bye—even if he went out to cut the grass. But, there was never any discussion of sex, jokes about sex, or idle conversation at the table about members of the congregation who had fallen into temptation.

Alas, many a pastor's son or daughter has become disillusioned about the church by ill-advised sharing of the temptations and sins of the parishioner during the evening meal. I shudder when I think of what my father's reaction would be to the openness with which sex is treated today, in the press and on TV.

In the 1920s I can recall only a few college graduates among us. Most were connected with the Bible Training School. Dean Olt, when he arrived in 1925, was the only faculty member to have a four-year college degree. Higher education at this period of time in the Midwest was available to perhaps four percent of high school graduates, with the result that there was no strong educational tradition going for us.

In particular, higher education was viewed with considerable suspicion as part of the reason for the apostasy of the church, a part of the "world" in these "latter days." Anderson Brown, C. E. Brown's brother, had earned a B.O. degree—Bachelor of Oratory—a bonafide four-year degree, but with end-times coming there was little need for educational credentials. Many a pastor chapel speaker in the 1930s announced right up front that he had earned a degree from the School of Hard Knocks.

The Isolated Life

As a child, and later as a teen-ager, I knew we were pilgrims in a strange land. The political world, higher education, the amusement world, the world of commerce, and entertainment were not for us. I always knew I did not belong there, but inside the church—in the Park Place, Gospel Trumpet community. This was my home, my world. We were God's people, we dwelt for only a brief time here in the world. Heaven was our home and our prayer was to make it. Marriage outside the church family was strongly discouraged. Even Art Hoffman forbade his girls to get serious with any boy unless he could sing at least four Church of God songs by heart.

Divorce rarely was a possibility if one intended to hold leadership in the church and there were very, very few who did. Pastors routinely refused to perform marriage ceremonies if either of the couple had been divorced. Premarital sex never was discussed as an option and a girl who had lost her virginity was "used merchandise." So sensitive were we against "the flesh" that mother would never use the word *legs*. *Limbs* was used as a substitute on rare occasions. All things considered, our Victorian views of sex—keep it under wraps as long as possible; say as little about it as necessary—were not open and healthy. I used to sing "the days of sex and creeds for us forevermore is passed" until I learned better. Beloved Carl Kardatzke did more than anyone else to open the doors for a wholesome dialogue on sex.

In my preteen years, I was fascinated much more with cars than sex. We often drove past the Packard Agency in Denver in our used Nash and saw those magnificent automobiles, arrayed in all their splendor, through the showroom windows. I knew every car on the road and what year it was made; I had small models stashed away in a box for safekeeping and filled them with hot paraffin to make them run heavier and coast longer.

Bill was a born engineer and mechanic. When we bought the 1927 Nash, he had the engine torn down, grinding the valves, in our basement at 4627 Moncrieff, before we had owned it a week. He was about sixteen at that time. The old 1924 Studebaker touring car, which we traded in on the Nash, was an abomination to mother. It had a reinforcing rib supporting the canvas top, just above the back passenger seat where mother frequently sat. When dad crossed a railroad crossing, the old Studebaker had a way of bucking sharply and kicking mother upward, cracking her head on this rib. She let father know in no uncertain terms how she felt.

That Love for Autos

I began my life-long romance with cars, being corrupted by another car buff, Steele C. Smith. Steele always drove the flashy ones. One year he came to camp meeting, when I was about twelve, took me for a ride in a bright red Marmon, and actually let me drive it out Tenth Street to Rangeline Road. After that, Steele let me drive a whole series of Marmons, Buicks, Cadillacs, Pierce Arrows, down to recent years. One thing Steele learned from his years pastoring in Boston and taking some classes at Harvard was "The importance of class!" Some rubbed off on me, so I was humiliated to be dropped off at Anderson High School in our ancient green 1928 Chrysler, whose squeaking brakes announced our poverty for blocks around. But, pay as you go was not a way of life to be put away easily.

This 1928 green Chrysler was nearly my undoing. Dad was away preaching and mother let me drive the car to high school on a spring day after a snow that had melted the streets bare—except where the shadow of Sam Bathauer's grocery store protected the ice at Fifth and College. Parked on the south side of Fifth, three or four car-lengths from the corner, was Brother Nisely's plumbing truck with a large assortment of pipe sticking out the back. Coming around the corner I lost it on the ice. Around came the rear end, smashing into the back of the truck. When I extricated the old Chrysler she was still intact, but about twenty holes had been punched in her rear side and back. It took all my savings to get the old girl leaded up and painted before father got back home.

I was fourteen when we packed up and left Denver to return to Anderson. We put the house up for sale and, while I was alone in the house one Saturday afternoon, our first prospects arrived. I showed them through, told them the price—about $3,700—extolled the virtues of the neighborhood, and clinched the deal before mom and dad came home. We gave possession on June 1, 1933, and moved in with Brother and Sister John Maring for several weeks. The Marings were German-speaking Swiss immigrants who ran a vegetable farm on Sheridan Street. They lived in a fine old brick farm-house with a front gate and a lane leading back to the barn. We knew and loved these dear people, and parting was not easy.

Back to Anderson

The Marings treated us like family till it was time to leave for Anderson. I recall the last day clearly. Trunks were strapped and secured to the running boards, clothing packed, suitcases ready. We rose at 2:30 A.M., had a farm breakfast, said good-bye, and started down the drive to the gate. Old Brother Maring had gone ahead to open it. There he stood, tall, rawboned, ruddy complexioned, holding his ten-gallon hat over his heart; tears were running down his cheeks. Although I was just a boy, that scene has stayed with me. It has spoken to me again and again of the deep feeling and special relationship of love that exists between a loving and trusted pastor and members of the flock.

Although I grew up in a minister's home. I never resented it, and, if I could turn the clock back and had the chance, I would not change a thing. The church during these times had gravitated to a highly prescriptive life-style of external things by which sanctification and the spirit-filled life was measured. Some of my friends felt imprisoned, resentful and, when independence came, left the church never to return. Although we also lived in this environment, our parents gave us room. In junior high I was permitted to attend some school-sponsored films, and the rules and regulations began to soften. The big factor in the equation was warmth and love. The harsh spirit of fanaticism never was a part of our lives. We had all we needed: parents who loved and supported us, good health, music lessons, family fun, travel, and an atmosphere of peace and security. We often pushed hard against the constraints of the church, but we never turned away.

I never was inside a barbershop until we returned to Anderson in the 1930s. Saturday night was hair cutting. Father had his mind and heart on the

Sunday sermons and his patience often was thin. I hated to sit quietly on a stool in the furnace room while he clipped away with old clippers that did more than cut. Once in a while it yanked out a few hairs, much to my displeasure. Admonitions to "hold still," "don't turn your head away," "sit up straight" were frequent. Often mother was close by to offer suggestions. When it was over she insisted that I say, after enduring all this misery, "Thank you, daddy." I solemnly vowed to spare my own children this indignity. But, saving a quarter was very important for us in those days.

In the 1930s the depression was on: few had jobs. Father was paid twelve dollars per week total; he had a part-time secretary, Gertrude Little, and a church custodian, J. W. Phelps, who had retired as secretary of the Missionary Board. Phelps was a socialist who often lectured me on the advantages of government ownership when I came over to practice the organ.

Dancing and going to the prom were not for Church of God students. The prom was the big social event of the year at Anderson High School. My memories of the 1936 AHS prom still are very real. I did not attend first, because I knew it would be futile to ask for permission; second, because I knew if I were to sneak off, my parents would find out and it would be hard for father to handle; and, third, because I did not know how to dance.

The major arguments offered by our Sunday school teachers against dancing were that dances brought together worldly, unsaved people where mingling led us astray. It was argued that the proximity of bodies inflamed passionate instincts and left young people out of control, carried away by inhibitions, and it led to sexual promiscuity. Tracts were available. One was titled *From the Ballroom to Hell.* In our high school youth fellowship we had more than fifty teen-agers. Only two or three crossed the line and attended the prom. In all fairness, our leaders at Park Place made very little of it, and we loved our parents too much to go against them. In time the youth department planned a prom substitute—a big dress-up banquet for nonattenders. Soon this fizzled when half of the group left early to attend the prom.

In my case I got permission to use our new 1936 Studebaker for the evening, went by and picked up my friend, Mona Morrison, and drove around. It was not very exciting just driving around, so we decided to head for the high bluff where the pavement ended on West Ninth Street. We picked up speed as we approached, shot off the pavement into space, and came down hard, scooping up dirt as we landed in the tracks that led up the steep incline to the top. We made it and it provided some real excitement. The next morning father called me out to look at the radiator grill. All the chrome vertical braces had been bent out of shape where we had dug into the dirt. It was a sorry and expensive sight. Better I should have gone to the prom. Father only shook his head. I paid.

High School Antics

While I was in high school I carried the Anderson Daily Bulletin to 220 homes and to the downtown drugstores. The weekly rate was 15 cents of which I received 4 cents. I shall never forget what it was like to try to get 220 copies of the Bulletin in my bag, especially on nights when the paper ran to 24 pages, lugging the lot across the old Eighth Street bridge when the thermometer read below zero and the wind howling down from the North. I carried the newspaper whether I felt like it or not, dealt with deadbeats, paid the office each week, and learned to fold and sail a newspaper with unerring accuracy. So, I had my own money to spend, and all during high school I paid for all my clothes, entertainment, books, and school supplies myself. Furthermore, I learned how to get along with customers and how to be responsible in running a small business. After my inauguration as president of Anderson College in 1958, one of my customers came up to say "I don't care much about this new job you've got, but you'll always be my paper boy."

Most of us do some very dumb things during our high school days. Coming home one day In the early winter I noticed the river was frozen over as we came to the old Tenth Street bridge. My buddies warned me but I was determined to cross the river on the ice to see If skating was possible. As I got to the middle, there was a sharp crack and I fell into the icy water whose swift current pulled and dragged at my heavy clothing, threatening to drag me under. Fortunately I was able to cling to the ice and make my way toward shore, breaking off large chunks till I was able to climb out.

On another day, Mark Bright and I took out his parent's 1934 Chevy to see how fast it would go. Coming along, wide open, on Lindberg Road we saw the old Alexandria Pike crossing come into the view as the speedometer hit the 85-mph mark.

Mark hit the brakes and we began to slide, the car skidding and tipping dangerously as we shot backwards across the Pike and deep into the drive of the house across the road. We paused for a moment, got ourselves together, went home, and put on some dry pants.

Dating represented the possibility of some exitement but it was a game one had to play with considerable restrictions. Mother once took me aside, looked up at me with those serious dark brown eyes and said, "Bob, I know you'd never lay your hand on a girl." I had some trouble with this. On Sunday some of us pushed our Sunday school class teacher to the absolute limit in describing just what was possible. Fortunately, most of us stayed within the limits and survived. I know my parents rarely got to sleep till I got in. Eleven o'clock was the deadline. Who you were with and where you were going was required information. To my chagrin, the squeaking back stairs always gave me away when I was late. But, dating was great fun; to be close, to listen to the car radio and the quiet rich voice of the poet and his music. "Moon river, enchanted white ribbon, 'twined in the hair of night. . . ." Golden memories.

During my years at Anderson High School my closest friends were Mark Bright, Melvin "Buck" Thornburg, and Everett Beck. At the end of the summer of 1936 we made one more trip to East Side Jersey Dairy for a thick milkshake and said "so long" to each other. Mark went on to DePauw on a Rector Scholarship, Everett and Buck to Indiana University, and I to Anderson College. Little did we know what the coming years held for us. Mark was shot down in flames in the South Pacific, Buck became an Anderson attorney, and Everett Beck a respected doctor in Indianapolis.

9

What about College?

In the 1930s, going to Anderson College was nothing to brag about in the eyes of Anderson people. The institution was not accredited, had poor facilities and was considered locally as a Bible school preacher factory for Church of God students only. In 1932 it had graduated its first liberal arts class. The depression was just beginning to lift but pulling out of the economic morass was difficult and there were few signs of optimism about.

Two things I never questioned. I knew I was going to go to college, and I knew it would be at Anderson. Father said to give it my best for two years and then I could consider a change. My brother had had two years at the University of Colorado and transferred to Purdue in engineering, so had good reason for bypassing Anderson College, but I knew in my bones that it was better to cooperate with the inevitable. So, in the fall of 1936 I presented myself, more or less willingly, as a student—but elected to stay in my room at home, eat mom's cooking, and have somewhat more freedom to move about. Home was five short blocks from campus and my room, a gathering place for college brothers fleeing from the austerity of Old Main.

As I reflect back on 1936, I recall gathering in the chapel in Old Main, the abandoned Gospel Trumpet Company Worker's Home. We were not an impressive sight. All told, full-time, part-time, special students, and those auditing, we would have been hard pressed to total two hundred. The great depression still stalked the land, leaving few families with money to send their children to college. Few students arrived with any money, jobs were scarce, and faculty were getting three-hundred to five-hundred dollars per year, if they could collect it. This gave rise to an elaborate bartering system of trading in kind, which circumvented the need for cash. During these years the college truck roamed the Midwest picking up potatoes, nonperishable items, and an occasional side of beef from friendly congregations. One year we got loaded with sauerkraut, pervading the hill with its pungent perfume. Those were tough days when giving up and closing up would have been easy.

But, there were other problems to deal with. The college had just two years before concluded a monumental confrontation with conservative elements in the church who wanted a change of administration and a return to the Bible Training School. This was no minor skirmish. It divided the strongest leaders, dumped suspicion and mistrust on the college leadership, and exhausted pastors and congregations in a life and death struggle—a confrontation chronicled in my book *The Early Morning Light,* and in Dr. John A. Morrison's *As the River Flows.*

So in the fall of 1936 the potshots were still coming. Some wanted the college to indoctrinate students in reformation theology. Some wanted it to be a training program for pastors and evangelists exclusively. Some parents thought it a safe haven for an education, isolated from upsetting ideas and evil companions, and others figured it a good place to find a mate.

Yet, the president and dean, the dozen full- and part-time faculty saw a different vision and held to it with a passion and determination that still moves me profoundly. For them, the life of the mind, the great literature of the Western world, the expanding horizons of science, the insights of philosophy and psychology, all were a legitimate part of our educational birthright and should be available to young people growing up in the Church of God.

The Framework of Faith

But this was not all. These great disciplines of the mind were not enough to give health and direction to society. Even a spirit of freedom to think and question, and a thorough grounding in the classic liberal arts curriculum were not enough. Something else was needed, a transcending framework of faith to give education a compelling sense of direction and meaning for life.

No one articulated this more regularly or with more passion than did our president. Furthermore, there on the platform in that austere chapel, with its small faculty sitting in a semicircle, there we saw before us men and women committed to this great vision, willing to sacrifice financial gain for the ancient vision of Christ's great mission on earth and for the kind of Christian higher education essential to make us intelligent participants in that mission. Their dedication to that cause inspired us, lifted our sights, and saved us from self-pity. Those before us—John Morrison, Dean Russell Olt, Amy Lopez, Carl Kardatzke, Earl Martin, Otto Linn, Walter Haldeman, and others—were drawn together by the vision, following it joyfully, enduring the indignities of poverty without complaint. It is of such people and such vision that a strong sense of community is made. I did not take long to be caught up in its life.

Dr. Morrison on many occasions mentioned a long walk with my father, his confidant and pastor, on a miserably cold January afternoon, in the depths of the college's struggle to survive. They had walked along the railroad tracks out to the bridge across White River, Jackson's Crossing, turned round and walked in that deep silence born of love and understanding, till they reached the campus. They stopped for a moment to watch the lights come on in Old Main. "See those lights, J. A.?" my father asked. "We are never going to let them go out." It is now more than a half-century since that moment that meant so much to them both. The lights do still shine and thousands of graduates and former students testify to the centrality of their experience in a Christian college.

What *Social Life*?

Social life on campus was not only austere but practically nonexistent for a first-year student. The

74

rules were clearly spelled out and enforced by Dr. Vila Deubach, dean of women, and the awesome presence of Dean Russell Olt. The building was locked at 10:15 P.M. weeknights, no dating at all for freshmen and women till after Thanksgiving. Conversations between sexes were limited to three minutes, riding together in a car was forbidden, along with a long catalog of specific restrictions.

Dean Olt was an imposing figure, with a large frame. A scowl from his black eyes could bring terror to the heart of any transgressor. He presided over all academic affairs, seated on a highly pitched swivel throne. Visitors sat on arm chairs, whose legs had been sawed off, requiring them to gaze upward in a definitely subservient position. Students credited him with extrasensory powers that enabled him to ferret out the most closely guarded secrets. Sundays he disappeared to Cincinnati where he underwent a loving, gentle, complete personality change as pastor of one of our Church of God congregations.

Dean Olt, an academician, schooled in the German tradition, knew where he was headed, straight into the doors of the North Central Association, the accrediting agency in our area, and to this goal he gave his unbounded energy. Early on he familiarized himself with their standards and all academic decisions were ajudicated thereby. His reign of terror as a teacher began when he failed seventy-five percent of his freshmen psychology class in their six-weeks grades. His teaching methods were based on fear and intimidation, yet there was such an air of moral and academic greatness about the man that we grudgingly endured it all.

Students knew little about his organizing the Peace Fellowship, launching the Annual International Youth Convention, walking with the labor unions in a parade to legitimize their role in local General Motor plants, or acting to bring scores of displaced families to the U.S. after World War II. His passion was peace, brotherhood, and justice for laboring men and women.

Dean Olt was not an academic functionary to be taken lightly. He was law and gospel, more former than latter. Every school day during his office hours, students could be seen sitting outside his office waiting to explain some major or minor infraction of the rules. The ritual was the same. There was no secretary in an outer office with a kindly word of encouragement. One had to knock on the door. Then came a booming voice, like from Sinai, "Come!" Wes Neal, who had been to a late-night party, climbed into his room using the fire escape, and had ridden unchaperoned with his girlfriend in an automobile, was called on the carpet the following day. Assuming that the jig was up, he slumped down in the chair across from the dean and confessed his sin. After a thorough cleansing he paused waiting for the earth to shake and the thunder to roll. Instead, he heard the dean say, "Now, what I called you in about. . . ."

My most difficult experience came with Dean Olt over a term paper. I had written a paper for his psychology of religion class that was returned with a *B* and a note or two on the cover. The next year I signed up for his class on philosophy of religion and casting about for a term paper topic, I hit on a brilliant idea. Why not use last year's paper? Tear off the front page and replace it. The dean would never remember. It was a poor assumption. The paper came back with an *F* and a brief note in red ink, "See back page." There was last year's marginal note in his hand, "Idea needs to be expanded," which somehow I had over-looked. Back to square one after a strong lecture on honesty.

Dean Olt was a man far ahead of his time. He nearly always was in some sort of trouble. Because of his support of the unions, his pacifism, his support of black civil rights, and his rejection of narrow fundamentalism, he constantly was the object of criticism In a town in which no restaurant would serve a black person, nor was there a motel where a black person could sleep. A few of us knew this and admired him for it.

Those Chapel Sessions

In chapel there often were moments of high inspiration and times when the sublime gave way to the ridiculous. One of many such times was the day a functionary from the Indiana State Department of Education arrived to make a speech. As customary, chapel began with the reading of a psalm—in this case highly appropriate. "Make a joyful noise unto the Lord all the earth."

Before chapel, a few skallywags had slipped in, woven tissue paper through the piano strings, and planted an alarm clock inside the pulpit set to make an insistent suggestion to the speaker at an appropriate time. First, the introduction to the first hymn sounded like the piano in Melchers Tavern on the town square, causing Professor Cecil Hart-selle to rub his eye vigorously. Then in the midst of an impossibly dull speech the trusty alarm did its faithful work. A photograph of Dean Olt's face at the time would not have been aglow with Christian charity.

I often have asked myself why chapel was such an important part of college life. The gathering of the campus certainly was a regular social event. There were times of worship and stimulating speaking, and all important campus events were announced there. But it was more than this. We had a strong sense that we were the "different" ones. Different from the secular public colleges and universities, different from the standard denominational world, different from the "world" out there with its distorted values and material aspirations.

Although Dean Olt and President Morrison constantly challenged us to push back our cultural and intellectual horizons, they also fostered in us that as a community we belonged to God. We were to follow Christ's example of servanthood and not to be ashamed of an all-encompassing mission to be a part of God's great redemptive plan for the world.

We felt this often in that bare old room that had served as a place of worship by our forefathers and foremothers and their families. We felt it when we sat in the battle-scarred old opera chairs and when we stood together to sing and pray. Here was the place many of us moved from the constant probing and reaching of the classroom questions to the integrating, illuminating, confirming experience of the Christian faith. This faith shone in the faces around us, spoke to us in what our teachers were about, and fanned that spark of faith we had brought from home and church. Chapel called us back again and again to our Christian roots, and helped us to engraft ourselves in to that great tree of life. This is the pearl of great price for the Christian college. When the "heavenly vision" is gone, no magnificent buildings, libraries, credentials and accreditations will suffice. Even though we were small, unaccredited, and hung by a financial thread, we were rich in dreams.

When I was a freshman, seated in proper alphabetical order next to my friend Leslie Ratzlaff, I became increasingly apprehensive as the time to pray drew near, especially when Dean Olt presided. Would I be called on to lead in prayer? The thought of leading a public prayer before faculty and students started my heart pounding and made my mouth dry. The Dean always read the scripture first and *then*, with no warning, singled someone out to pray. I recall vividly one day in chapel being so frightened that I got up, rushed out, and did not return until this part of the worship was over. Another time when the Dean nailed me, I floundered around hopelessly and wound up with "O Lord er, ah, help us be walking billboards for Thee," which brought forth a loud snort from my friend Val Clear.

10

College and Seminary Days

Of course dreams of a better world were not all we were dreaming about. It was the time of life for romance and, in spite of the watchful eye of the administration, love found a way. When Jerry Hurst, of Princeton, Indiana, arrived on campus in the fall of 1939, this beautiful blue-eyed, blonde-haired creature set many a male heart pounding, mine being no exception. At Thanksgiving time I was still trying to beat out the opposition, sulking with jealousy when she went out with someone else. Jerry already was a sort of celebrity in the church having traveled widely as a girl evangelist, holding meetings in many of our larger congregations throughout the country.

It did not take long to overcome my prejudice against women evangelists, and by Christmas of 1939 I was completely and hopelessly in love. I was pleased that she had my picture in her dorm room and overjoyed when she took it home to show her father. He inspected the photograph carefully, laid it down with the comment, "Well, he has nice, big ears!" In the spring, late May 1940, we sat out under the great ash tree just east of Decker Hall and confessed our love to each other and, before school was out, met our friends over at the park in Noblesville to announce our engagement. I was too poor to buy a ring; anyway engagement rings were not acceptable. Instead, I gave Jerry a watch, which she still wears on occasion.

The courtship ritual at Anderson College among my close friends was very straight, exceedingly so by contemporary standards. No dancing, no drinking, no partying, no premarital sex, no drugs, no heavy petting and in spite of it all, romance flourished. The college was a close, tight, community and most of us knew what was going on among our friends and in the student body. To use a contemporary term, we were not sexually active. On very rare occasions a girl became pregnant, or a boy was sent home for promiscuous behavior, but standards were strict and for the most part accepted and obeyed. Extraordinarily helpful to students was Dr. Carl Kardatzke who made talking about sexuality an open and legitimate subject in a puritanical environment.

Testing the Limits

Always among us were those students who were testing the limits. Although there was a ban on smoking, a group of male students decided to test the validity of this rule from a religious perspective. They established the smoker's prayer meeting, carrying out their clandestine activities in a house up on High Street, where they met to pray and smoke.

It could be done, they reported, until the dean put their fire out.

Since Val Clear, Carol Helvey, and I were convinced that Jesus had not turned the water into Welch's grape juice, we ventured over to a Noblesville tavern one night to prove to ourselves that drinking was no sin. It must have been cheap gin or else the fear that my sin would be found out. I threw up on the way home.

And then there was the December night six of us piled into a car, drove to Indianapolis, and wound up at the burlesque. I still recall the filthy, run-down theater, the sense of shame and guilt, the shocking language, and lewd dancing. Halfway through, we stood up, walked out, feeling thoroughly defiled. There, under the theater marquee in the bitter subzero cold, was the Salvation Army, huddled together around the iron pot, playing hymns of grace and redemption, peace and goodwill. Each one of us emptied his pockets. I lied to my father about what had transpired and had to enter the secret closet confessional a number of times before the nagging sense of guilt went away and absolution came from above.

As I look back on my college days at Anderson College I regret the absence of a community of black students with which to interact. In the 1930s only a small percentage of minority high school graduates went on to college and few had the money or the incentive. Black students at Anderson could be counted on the fingers of one hand. The cause of equal opportunity was pressed constantly by Dean Olt but we were really isolated from black people except when large numbers came to camp meeting. Interracial dating would have posed a major campus problem. This isolation represents a major loss in my formative years, one that I regret. But the Missionary Home, around I900-1910 in Chicago, was integrated, and a sizable number of black brothers and sisters attended the congregation that met in the chapel there. To this group who felt a need to establish their own congregation, my father was instrumental in bringing Dr. S. P. Dunn to the city as their first pastor.

Boosters and Flying

Prior to 1938 there were no social clubs on campus. I do not recall any direct prohibition against them, although serious questions might have been raised by those familiar with the fraternity and sorority system. But in 1938 some of us thought a club comprised of some of our friends might provide for a closeness and depth of fellowship that was lacking. We took over the athletic booster organization designed several years earlier by Ed May and the athletic department to cheer, yell, dispute calls and otherwise create support for the team. May's effort fizzled but left an organizational shell intact.

David Houghton, Mitt Williams, and I got things organized, wrote a constitution calling for a high sense of honor and fidelity to Anderson College forever, called our buddies together, swore them in, and declared ourselves the Boosters, cream of the crop. We stole our club song *We're all Pals Together*, from Victor Herbert and proceeded to send off for large orange As and black sweaters. In a few weeks we were off and running, singing lustily, and strutting about the campus in our flashy sweaters.

Trouble developed quickly. An immediate protest arose from athletes who had practiced long hours and played on court and field for the honor of Anderson College. Who were these guys awarding themselves the cherished athletic emblem without paying the price? We backed up quickly, took our lumps and forged on.

Almost at once a rival group organized by Byron Westlake called themselves the Sachem Club. For fifty years these clubs have competed against each other, sometimes in a friendly way, and at times in an unsanctified manner. Boosters sold candy, planned social events, claimed to champion good causes, held early morning hikes out to Jackson's Crossing and planned a big formal once per year. Some of the happiest memories of my college career grew out of this association and I was honored to serve as its first president.

In 1939 word came from the Civil Aeronautics Board, presided over by former Andersonian Oswald Ryan, that Anderson College would be awarded one of its first pilot training programs. Twelve of us signed up at once, working in the extra class work in the only time mutually available, 5:30 A.M. We studied navigation, meterology, and regulations governing flight, and we drove out each day to take flight instruction at the old Anderson Airport, now the site of Target Shopping Center. We did stalls, spins, power turns, shot landings; it opened up a whole wonderful exciting world. I shall not forget my solo flight, front seat conspicuously empty as I took off into the sky, circled and landed the bright yellow "J" Cub.

Later I flew to Indianapolis, after piling up the

required solo hours, to be examined for my license. In the spring of 1940 I took the inspector for a ride, passed the test with flying colors, and claimed my private pilot's license. Not long afterward I rented a plane and took my closest friend, Mark Bright, for his first plane ride. We flew north and west to Elwood where Wendell Willkie was making his hometown bid for the presidency. The town was overflowing with great crowds of people as we circled overhead. Mark was so entranced by the ride that he joined the navy and flew a Grumman Hell Cat to his death in World War II near Sipan in the South Pacific.

11

Call to Christian Service

During my junior year at Anderson College a part of me began to sense that I had some gifts that might fit me for the ministry. Another part of me took strong exception. My father, in his wisdom, never once spoke or urged me toward this calling. The year 1938 was a time of great struggle as I kept asking myself what I should be planning for the future. I recall being rather ashamed to let it be known that I was not sure, and I was not able to bring myself to a place of unqualified commitment to whatever God might have in mind for me.

One Sunday night I was seated by the organ, up front in Park Place church, listening to W. E. Monk talk about all the congregations scattered around the country that did not have pastors. Somehow I managed to store this bit of information away in my mind and it suggested to me there was a need here that I might be able to meet. Perhaps I might be able to serve some small, remote congregation out there in desperate circumstances. This Sunday night service and its ancient challenge that the "harvest is great but the laborers few," impacted my thinking. It is important that at this time I would have resisted any pressure to declare for the ministry. Other voices were calling and I did not want anyone to tell me what to think, whom to marry or what vocation to follow, a trait that still has its stubborn roots deep in the soil of my life.

Father was sensitive to this and never urged the ministry on me, but early in my junior year at Anderson I felt that I was being drawn to a moment of decision. So, late one night, sitting up pondering this whole issue of vocation, the thought came to me that my call as a Christian was to say a simple yes to whatever God had in mind. When the good heavenly Father led me gently to this gate, I summoned up all my courage, said *yes*, and walked through.

This unconditional *yes* brought a profound sense of peace to my struggling heart. I look back on it as a time like John Wesley's experience at Aldergate, when his heart was "strangely warmed." So, my own heart responded to God's intimate and illuminating presence. It was there that I knew God's visitation in a special way, knew that God does come to us in special moments. I went to my room with a sense of peace. The conflict was over. God was calling me. God had something in mind; now my response was to listen and obey. From that moment on, the ministry as a vocation began to take hold and confirmation grew stronger with each passing day.

The liberal arts curriculum at Anderson, presided over by Dean Olt, was no pushover. It mandated strong doses of science, history, literature, psychology, philosophy, foreign language, and religion. My majors were both English and psychology, with a minor in history. I have always been grateful for this. The curriculum opened up the world of arts and letters, science, social sciences, and history, which were a wonderful foundation for further study.

Off to Oberlin

In the summer of 1938 I went to Oberlin to study the pipe organ at the conservatory and attend summer school in the college. The experience at Oberlin was an important one for me, because it gave me a chance to study the organ seriously in one of the nation's most prestigious conservatories, noted for its excellent organ department.

For the first time I began to practice many hours a day. I worked on the classics, Vidor, Bach, Boellman, Franck, and enjoyed playing the exciting instruments in Finney Chapel and the music hall. In addition there were courses in philosophy and economics, which gave me a chance to broaden my intellectual horizons in a new environment. I lived with Dan and Esther Martin and attended the rural Kipton Community Church, which Dan pastored as a seminary student. I am sure this experience influenced my decision to enroll in the Oberlin Graduate School of Theology and to become pastor of the Kipton Community Church in the fall of 1941.

At the end of the summer of 1938 I went to Milwaukee to attend the International Youth Convention. There I met Jerry for the first time and had a strong sense that somehow our lives might be drawn together. Unfortunately she was not so

89

affected and would have nothing to do with me. She did turn up on campus that fall, however, and the self-fulling prophecy began to take shape.

Other summers I spent working as a carpenter for Russell Byrum. I worked first on a framing crew and later putting on cedar siding. Today I pass houses I helped build. I got paid forty cents per hour, squirreled it away in Anderson Bank for the fall, and enjoyed the experience of working with my hands. There were no power tools. One morning Jack VanDyke and I spent the entire five hours sawing studs only to have Mr. Byrum discover they were sawed off several inches short. There is no device that will stretch a two by four and we were admonished by a disgusted, but silent, gaze from Mr. Byrum.

One college in Indiana, years ago, listed in its catalog that it was located "ten miles from any known form of sin." Anderson was not so located. The village brothel was only a matter of a few blocks away, where Eighth Street passed under the Pennsylvania Railroad tracks, and the opportunity for evil never was far away. But Anderson College was indeed a sheltered place as far as dens of wickedness go. When my friend Mark Bright came home from DePauw, he told stories of fraternity mischief that opened my eyes. But, even at that time, Anderson was not sheltered from ideas. Dean Olt and John Morrison saw to that. They were devoted to academic freedom, and so we were spared the narrow, fundamentalist, dogmatic approach to learning, particularly in matters of faith and conduct. I always shall be grateful for this, especially since it was a day in which indoctrination tended to be fairly rigid among our church constituents whose support was paying for our education. I later learned first-hand how vital it is to keep the doors and windows of freedom open to students.

War on the Horizon

By the fall of 1938 the papers were bringing foreboding news of Hitler's activities in central Europe. I recall an increasingly uneasy feeling about the prospect of war and being drawn into it. Particularly among our closest friends the subject came up, and many "what if" questions got a great deal of attention. I recall sitting in one of the student lounges listening to the strident voice of Hitler and the roar of thousands of Nazi storm troopers as they shouted their support. I read his *Mein Kampf* and put it down with a rock in my stomach.

Although the "peace witness" was not a part of our theological root system, still, Christian literature, quarterlies, and so forth, were filled with lessons on the follies of war and its horrendous cost in dollars and human suffering. In the Midwest, traditionally isolationist, the sentiment was strong for staying out. Most of us were hoping that some peaceful solutions could be found and listened to the reports of Neville Chamberlain as he shuttled between London and Berlin. Tom Rowe, one of my closest friends, after a serious discussion in which all of us had declared we would not go and fight, stood up and said he was not ready to declare himself, that circumstances change and that people do also. Tom was killed on a beach during the North Africa invasion a few years later.

When I graduated from college in 1940, my life was coming together. I was finishing my under-graduate degree, was engaged, had won my pilot's license, had made a strong vocational commitment to the ministry, and had been admitted to the Oberlin Graduate School of Theology.

My roommate Warren Edmondson and I were assigned quarters in Bosworth Hall and I was fortunate to be able to earn my board, room, and tuition playing the fine pipe organ in Fairchild Chapel. Both Warren and I were eager to get started in ministry and prevailed on our friend Warren Roark, a leading pastor in Canton, to help us land a church to serve. With his help we managed in invitation to the Church of God in Loudon-ville.

We rode the bus down to the center of town on Saturday but could not locate the place. After much inquiry we discovered that the congregation met at Walter VanScroder's house, three miles from town, back up in the hills. After a good night's rest with this gracious family we were ready to meet the congregation, which filled the parlor and sat expectantly to hear what those two young preach-ers had to offer. Being hard up for leadership, they invited us to pastor the church with a stipend of five dollars to split between us. Any free-will dona-tions were to be credited against the five.

As I reflect on this experience I marvel at the forbearance of these good people. As we drove down each week from the ivory towers of Oberlin and the educational sophistication of the seminary and its world-renowned scholars, we were soon immersed in a radically different world, and it was good for us. When the year ended, the attendance had increased considerably, and we managed to move into a modest building erected by members of the congregation, near the highway where it stands today.

During the year F. G. Smith was gracious enough to ask me to come down to preach for him in the great church at Akron, Ohio. I rode the bus down and fell into conversation with an attractive, handsomely dressed man and his bejeweled wife. "What did I do? "I'm a minister in the Church of God, but of course we are nonpentecostal, don't speak in tongues; we frown on that sort of thing." "What do you do?" I asked. He replied, "I'm a minister." "What church?" "The Assembly of God," he replied. It was a long ride to Akron in which to contemplate my ineptitude. Brother Smith was amused by the story.

Wedding Plans Ahead

With the end of my first year in seminary in 1941 plans were beginning to shape up fast. Plans needed to be made for a wedding in August, and I needed to find a summer job. Warren Edmundson, my roommate and copastor had agreed that he would stay with the Loudonville congregation, and I would try to find another preaching assignment.

While hitch-hiking up from Ashland one day, I had an earnest talk with the Lord about these matters, and I had hardly finished my prayer when a car stopped and I found myself riding along with the personnel manager of the U.S. Steel Mill in Lorain. "What are you planning to do this summer?" he asked.

"Looking for a job," I said.

"Want to work in the mill?"

"You bet," I answered.

"It is tough, dirty work, dangerous at times, but it pays well," he said.

When the spring semester was out, I went to work at the mill as a brakeman on the narrow-gage railroad pulling red-hot five-ton ingots from one stop to another, watching the fountain of sparks fly into the night sky from the great blast furnace, and contemplating the bars and rods of steel swinging on the crane overhead. Working in this environment, listening to colorful talk of the rank and file steel workers, was a baptism into the real world heretofore lacking in my somewhat sheltered environment. I thanked God for the experience, joined the union, saved my earnings, and dreamed of the day in late August when Jerry and I would begin our lives together.

One bright Sunday morning in midsummer, I rode my bicycle five miles west to attend the Kipton Community Church and learned that the official board was holding a meeting following the service to discuss finding a part-time pastor. Having made the acquaintance of a number of friends in the congregation from my summer at the conservatory, I asked if I could be considered. Again my prayers opened the door and I was offered the position for fifteen dollars per week and a plot to make a garden. Praise the Lord! Plans were falling into place.

Mid-July left only five weeks before the wedding, and I urgently needed to make a fast trip home to talk final wedding plans and to purchase a wedding ring. Many will think it curious that the latter could be a problem, but the majority of women in my home congregation did not wear a wedding band. I think many longed to, but plainness, the absence of worldly adornment, and the preaching against the wearing of gold was still part of the discipline.

Having been liberated from these narrow ideas, I dipped into Cousin's Jewelry and came home to show my mother a gold band with a tiny diamond in it. My mother had not been liberated, and the dark look on her face let me know that she was asking herself how this would play among the saints. To restore peace I returned the ring and returned with a plain gold band. Whoops—too flashy. So, back to Cousin's for a slim band that finally made the grade—but only with great reluctance.

On August 24, a beautiful Sunday morning, Jerry and I were married in my father's church at Park Place, in Anderson. It was a part of the regular Sunday morning service, I in my white suit and Jerry looking lovely in her long wedding gown. Here we were before God, surrounded by family, loved ones, and a thousand friends in the congregation, responding to the ancient charges and pledges, repeating the vows, listening to my father-pastor asking God to bless and prosper our union. And while the prayer of benediction came, and all eyes were closed—on went the ring. It did occur to me that I had little more to offer my bride then my father did in the missionary home thirty years earlier.

Pearl Harbor

Pearl Harbor fell like an unbelievable nightmare on the country. The atmosphere changed dramatically and with it our lives changed as well. Pearl

Harbor galvanized the nation, and the country put aside all else to pursue the war effort. Most of my close friends were either drafted or enlisted. So, when graduation loomed in June 1943, I had a major life decision to make. The navy was clamoring for chaplains. I knew my educational credentials would qualify me, but there was a nagging uneasiness in my mind about supporting the war effort with the blessing of the Prince of Peace. Still, my friends were out there, fighting and dying to turn back the monstrous evil of Nazi Germany.

In a quandary I went before the Lord, laid out matters to the U.S. Navy in the faith that if this was what God had in mind, then, so be it. Jerry agreed. So, I enlisted as a navy chaplain at the recruiting and induction center in Cleveland, in June of 1943. Although my enlistment was carried to the top in Washington, I was rejected because of allergy problems for which I had been taking medical treatment at the Cleveland Clinic. I am sure this was a major turning point in my life. I accepted the decisions as the hand of God in my affairs and went on. I looked for the open door and found it in a small, struggling congregation in Brookhaven, Pennsylvania, near Philadelphia. Jerry and I entered it expectantly and began the next years with a deep sense of gratitude to God. But that is another story.

Epilogue

In writing these reflections on coming of age between the two world wars I am beginning to get some perspective on the people and events that have shaped my life. There is no question but that we were poor. Luxuries were rare in our home, and Church of God pastors never expected anything else. Although we lived very much in the world—school, play, books—there was a quiet pervasive feeling that this world was not our home. To live otherwise was to adopt a secular view of life built on the pursuit of pleasure and the accumulation of material possessions. This radical view of how the world was to be viewed was a far cry from the hucksters of Madison Avenue and the flesh merchants of Hollywood. It was poverty of soul and spirit that was to be feared.

I often reflect the love and affection, the touching, the reaching out to each other, the encouragement, and the atmosphere free of suspicion and distrust that made such rich soil in which to grow. This was true not only in our home but in the church as well. The North Denver and Park Place congregations were nurturing congregations, healthy, supportive of children and young people. We belonged. We were part of a community where our names were known. We shared in its mysteries, its particular ways, its celebration, its laughter, and its tears.

I prize growing up in a home where there were transcendent values, the simple acceptance of the presence of the Lord, the unquestioned authority of primary biblical directives for living the Christian life, the supportive power of prayer and love within a framework of discipline. I observed in my parents a commitment to something far greater than material values, and I saw this demonstrated again and again. We are slowly beginning to realize today that our deepest values grow out of the soil of faith and obedience to the God who holds us accountable for the way we live and how we use what we are entrusted with.

I am thankful for a home that prized good music, books, periodicals, interesting table conversation, and a passion for learning. Although Anderson College in the 1930s was unaccredited and certainly not the Harvard of the Midwest, still it was not narrow, rigid, or doctrinaire. Its faculty had a passion for interaction with students, pushing them to test and examine, urging them to expand their intellectual horizons. I owe more to them than I'll ever know.

As I look back I can now testify to how tenderly and patiently God works in our lives. I see the hand of God guiding, quietly opening and closing doors, correcting, encouraging, illuminating the way even when I was unaware of it.

It was the Church of God that helped to shape my life during my early years and gave me a chance to be a part of its life now for seventy years.

It has given me a star to follow, a Savior to turn to, a friend to guide, a road to travel, a cause to live for, and a way to look beyond the material and the transient to the eternal and transcendent.